UNSENT LETTERS: HEALING AS I WRITE

FINDING HEALING IN THE WORDS WE NEVER SAID.

SNEHAL PADAYA

"To all who have carried the weight of unspoken words, may this book be a refuge—a place where silence finds its voice, emotions unfold without fear, and healing takes shape through the power of expression. May you discover the courage to release, the strength to embrace, and the wisdom to move forward. This journey is yours, and with every word, you reclaim your own story."

Contents

Acknowledgements

Writing a book is rarely a solitary endeavour—it is a journey shaped by countless moments of inspiration, encouragement, and support from others. As I reflect on the creation of this book, I am reminded of the many people who have played a part in my life, guiding me, uplifting me, and helping me grow. This space is dedicated to expressing my heartfelt gratitude to all those who have been a part of this journey.

To the **readers** of this book: thank you for opening your hearts to these words. Your willingness to engage with this journey gives it purpose and meaning. This book is as much yours as it is mine, and I hope it offers you the same clarity, peace, and inspiration it brought me.

To my **family**: thank you for your endless patience and understanding. Your presence has been my foundation through all the highs and lows.

To my dear friend **Adiba**: your motivation and creativity have been a light in my life. Seeing you write your books inspired me to embark on this journey, and for that, I am deeply grateful.

To my school, **Dominic Savio Vidhyalaya**, and my loving **teachers**: thank you for making my school years such a joyful and enriching chapter of my life. Those years remain a cherished part of my journey, filled with love, learning, and unforgettable memories that shaped me deeply to become who I am today and laid the foundation for my future.

To my college, **Smt. P. N. Doshi Women's College**, the **SPRJK Trust**, as well as my wonderful **teachers**: thank you for always encouraging me to push forward, guiding me to improve, and believing in my potential. Your support has been instrumental in shaping my path.

To my scholarship donors, the **LBW Trust and WFC Trust**: I am deeply grateful for your financial support during my college years, as well as the mentorship and improvement programs that helped me grow and discover myself. The skills and experiences I gained through your programs and certifications significantly contributed to my writing journey and shaped who I am today.

To all whose kindness, strength, or stories have touched my life—thank you for inspiring me to write. Whether through your support or the challenges you brought into my path, you've given me reasons to reflect, grow, and find the courage to express my emotions through these pages.

Your presence, in moments of light and hardship, has shaped this book into what it is. Through you, I've come to understand the power of vulnerability, the importance of resilience, and the healing that comes with embracing the entirety of life's journey.

With love and gratitude,

Snehal.

PREFACE

There are moments in life when emotions become too tangled to express, when words sit heavy on the heart but never find their way. **Unspoken feelings do not simply fade—they build within us, growing heavier with time until their weight is impossible to ignore.** The longer we hold onto unspoken words, the more they quietly shape us—until we are no longer carrying them, but they are carrying us.

These letters are born from those moments—the ones filled with silence, hesitation, and unspoken words. They are remnants of friendships that faded, love that was lost, lessons learned late, and closure that was never granted.

I began writing these letters not to send them, but to free myself from the weight of unresolved emotions. In every word, I discovered healing. In every sentence, I found understanding. Writing became my **way of reclaiming my voice**, of making sense of heartache, of transforming loss into growth. Each letter helped me navigate my own healing journey, offering clarity where once there was confusion.

This book is not just a collection of letters—it is a **guide, a reflection, and a conversation**. Within these pages, you will encounter experiences that may feel familiar, emotions that may echo your own, and guidance to help you embrace healing in your own way. More than just reading these words, you will be invited to explore your own path—to write, reflect, and process the emotions you have carried, because healing begins when we permit ourselves to do so.

To truly engage in this journey, you will find dedicated pages throughout the book—spaces where you can write your own unspoken words, release the emotions you have held onto, and take an active step toward healing. These moments of self-expression will transform this book into more than just a collection of reflections; they will make it a **personal sanctuary for your own growth.**

If you've ever held onto words you couldn't say, if you've ever longed for closure that never came, if you've ever wondered whether healing was possible—let this be your space to begin. **This journey is yours now, and every word is a step forward.**

Prologue

Dear Readers,
This creative non-fiction book is more than just a collection of letters—it's an invitation for you to reflect, connect, and express yourself. After each letter, you'll find highlighted Key Emotions inspired by the themes of the letters. They serve as inspiration, guiding you to explore memories and moments tied to them. You'll also find an Optional Prompt alongside the key emotions, designed to offer a bit of guidance if you'd like it.

Whether you choose to follow the prompt or draw inspiration from the emotions, there's no limit to how you decide to express yourself. You could write a letter, poem, journal entry, or even create something artistic—**whatever feels right to you**.

Writing is a powerful act of self-expression. It helps untangle thoughts, process feelings, and reconnect with moments you hold close. It's not just to release pain or negativity—reliving positive emotions like joy, love can bring clarity, warmth, & healing. Whether you use this space to explore complex emotions or celebrate uplifting ones, let it be your canvas for creativity and reflection.

There's no "right way" to write here—each expression you craft will be as unique as your experiences. Let your heart guide you, and embrace this journey of self-discovery and connection.
With Love,
Snehal.

UNSENT LETTERS

I

Echoes of the Unspoken Words

In This Part

We trace the quiet echoes of relationships and emotions left unspoken. Through letters to cherished connections and fading friendships, this part reflects on moments of tenderness, love, and longing that were never fully expressed. Each story invites you to revisit your own unspoken words and consider how silence shapes the bonds we hold dear.

Dear Nani,

My Gem, you are a presence I carry with me—not in vivid memories, but in feelings— a warmth that lingers and a love that transcends time. You were my guiding light, my quiet refuge, and my greatest protector—a bond I wish I could have held onto for longer.

It's not the details I remember clearly, but the essence of you. My memories of us are fragments, like scattered beams of soft sunlight streaming through a glass window. I recall sitting by your side, drawn not just to your company but to the simple joy of eating the peas you patiently peeled with a calm grace that only you could manage. That small act was filled with so much warmth, it remains etched in my heart to this day.

In that very moment, just as you stood up for me after Mom scolded me—I had been pleading for something trivial, perhaps a piece of stationery, which she had refused to buy me, saying I already had enough, which was quite true still being a child my sadness seemed unbearable until you chastised Mom in my defence. Whispering gently into my ear, you promised to make my little wish come true. True to your words, you walked with me to the shop and bought me exactly what I had asked for, regardless of whether it was necessary. You simply wanted to give me all that I wished for.

ॐ

Nani: (Noun) Maternal grandmother in Gujarati, one of many languages spoken across India.

Another memory rests heavily in my heart—the time I visited Mama's house when you were unwell. You were there, sitting on the sofa by the door, but something felt different. You didn't recognize me, and perhaps not even Mom, lost in the fog of your disease. I felt an ache I couldn't fully understand then—a child's confusion over a love that seemed momentarily lost.

And then came the last time I saw you, lying there at Mama's house after you had passed. I was too young to comprehend the depth of that moment or the weight of what death truly meant. It felt like standing before a quiet tide, its significance washing over me in waves I couldn't yet grasp, leaving me with a sense of something precious slipping away.

Even after you were gone, your presence stayed with me in unexpected ways. On a trip, after being bullied by someone who wanted me to be his girlfriend, I broke down in tears. When Mom tried to console me, I couldn't admit the truth and instead cried out that I missed you. In that moment, you became the safe haven my heart instinctively reached for.

During that time, when I was deeply immersed in horror shows, and one afternoon, a gust of wind opened the bedroom door. Without thinking, I said, "Hi Nani." I told

Mama: (Noun) Maternal uncle (mother's brother) in Gujarati, one of many languages spoken across India.

mom you were visiting—my young mind not yet grasping the truth—that you were already gone. Looking back, it feels foolish—but it was hope over fear.

Now, as I reflect, I realize how much I've missed you. I don't often think of you, but when I do, it feels like a warm hug reaching across time. Your love surrounds me in those moments, filling the void life often leaves behind.

I wish I had been older when you passed, old enough to hold onto those moments we shared. I would have loved you with the same intensity, whether you remembered me or not, because your love, Nani, was unconditional.

If you were here today, I'm certain you would have been my greatest friend and my truest guide. You would have stood by me through every challenge and joy, always offering the love and wisdom that only you could provide.

Thank you, Nani, for being the warmth in my life—the love I hold onto when the world feels cold. You were, and always will be, my safe haven. Wherever you are, I hope you are smiling, happy, and surrounded by the love you deserve.

I miss you deeply and send you all the love my heart can hold. I have loved you, and I always will.

Yours truly.

Reflection

Writing this letter reminded me of the extraordinary power of unconditional love—how it transcends time, illness, and even loss. It made me realize that the essence of someone we love can live on, not just in our memories, but in the warmth they leave behind within us. For anyone who has lost a loved one, the lesson here is to treasure the small, seemingly ordinary moments—the touch of a hand, the sound of a laugh, or the comfort of their presence.

Even when the details fade, the love you shared will remain, a guiding light in moments of doubt or sorrow. Hold onto that love as a source of strength, and let it remind you that the bonds we form with those who genuinely care for us never truly end. They continue to shape us, offering solace and guidance long after their physical presence is gone. Let this reflection encourage you to honour their memory by embracing the warmth they gave you and carrying it forward in your life.

Your Turn to Reflect

Key Emotions: Love, Warmth, Loss

Optional Prompt: Write about someone who made you feel safe, loved, and unconditionally cared for, or someone such that you lost.
Let your memories and feelings guide your words or creative expression.

To my childhood friends,

You were the ones who felt like home—the sisters I chose, or perhaps the sisters who chose me. For years, I thought we were inseparable, tied together by an unspoken understanding. And maybe we still are, though lately, I've begun to notice something shift, a quiet reminder that perhaps I was never the one being truly pampered.

For as long as I can remember, I was the one who majorly came to you—the one who reached out first, the one who asked when something seemed off, the one who stayed by your side when you needed me the most. I gave my all to our friendship, pouring myself into the moments that mattered, large or small. I noticed your sadness, your fears, the cracks you tried to hide. I noticed when you needed a push, when you needed reassurance, when you needed me. And I was there, wholeheartedly, unquestioningly.

I admired you not only for welcoming me with open arms when I was new, but for standing beside me through every high and low, all these years. You were there for me, and I will never forget that. But now, as I look back, I realize something that I had overlooked for so long—it was always me who came back. Even when I was the one who was hurt, even when you should have reached out first, it was always me who crossed the bridge, most.

With time, I've grown quieter, maybe more observant, or perhaps just more aware. I've wondered if I'm simply reading too much into it. I've thought about it endlessly—A LOT. But I can't ignore that when I stopped being the one to initiate, we began to drift. And it's not like I stopped completely, I still initiated, but small. I know life gets busy—studies, responsibilities, a million things pulling us in different directions. But the truth is, I was busy too. And yet, I still made YOU my priority. I stayed up late, multitasked, adjusted my world for you, never once asking for credit because that's how much you meant to me.

Now, as I see us growing apart, I can't help but feel the weight of it. It feels as though we are losing touch, little by little, and I fear that when I leave the country in a few months, our connection will only grow thinner. Even thinking about it hurts.

Still, no matter where life takes us, I will always hold onto the memories we created together—the laughter, the tears, the moments that shaped us. I'll always cherish those days and the role you played in my life, even if finding our way back to what we once were feels hard—but if you choose me, let it be freely, wholeheartedly, not out of habit or hesitation, but because you truly want to.

Wishing you all the love, happiness, and success in the world.

Yours truly.

Reflection

Friendships offer profound lessons—not just about their significance in our lives but about the beautiful balance of effort and connection. Writing this letter led me to a realization: the healthiest relationships thrive on mutual care and understanding. It's not about placing blame but about acknowledging when the scales shift and finding ways to nurture a more fulfilling connection.

The lesson here is about self-awareness—embracing the ebb and flow of friendships with grace and understanding. Cherish the memories, trust in the journey, and allow connections to evolve naturally. Some bonds will strengthen with mutual effort, while others may gently shift, leaving behind gratitude for what once was. By honoring your boundaries, you nurture space for relationships that bring balance, warmth, and genuine connection.

Your Turn to Reflect

Key Emotions: Friendship, Nostalgia, Longing

Optional Prompt: Reflect on a bond that brought comfort and joy into your life. Explore the emotions tied to the connection—whether it's the warmth of shared moments or the ache of growing apart.
Let the memories guide your thoughts.

To the Best Friend I Could Have Had,

It is only now, with time and hindsight, that I realize what I lost—and why. It was my ignorance, my misplaced focus, that led us apart. I've come to understand that we could have been the best of friends if only I had paused, stepped back from the chaos of chasing after someone else—a person who abandoned our friendship without specifying a reason—and given you the attention you truly deserved.

You were always there for me. You believed in me, thought of me as your best friend, and yet I failed to see the treasure of your presence. Instead, I hurt you—not intentionally, but by neglect. I let myself be consumed by a friendship that had crumbled, never noticing how my actions made you feel like an afterthought. How often must you have felt reduced to an option while I spoke endlessly of someone else? And all the while, I remained oblivious to the pain I caused.

I owe you an apology—not just for my distraction but for the way I failed to honour our bond. I regret every moment I overlooked your feelings and every time I made you doubt your place in my life. You were kind and patient with me when I was caught up in my emotional immaturity, clinging to someone who had abandoned me. And in my blind pursuit, I hurt you—someone far more precious than I ever realized in those moments.

Perhaps I was wrong to think my distraction was the only reason for your distance. Maybe there were other wounds I unknowingly caused. If so, I am deeply, sincerely sorry. I now see that I had no right to make you question whether to fight for our friendship or step away for your own well-being.

By the time I realized my mistake, it was already too late. You had started to drift away, and I was left trying to repair something I had broken. I tried to make amends, but the weight of guilt lingered. Every memory of us felt bittersweet—a reminder of the bond I had once taken for granted, even if unintentionally. The pink necklace you gifted me on my birthday, the Instagram posts I still revisit, the familiar places we once shared—all stir a mix of longing and regret. I think of the naive version of myself who chased after someone who had already left, instead of holding onto the one who stayed.

It breaks my heart to accept that it's hard to undo what has been done. I lost someone who was more than just kind-hearted—she was a rare soul, one of the truest, sweetest, and most humble—not just because of my ignorance, but also because of the pain I inflicted. And now, I find myself wondering—do you ever think of me? Do you ever pause to revisit my posts or relive the moments we shared? As I write this, the question lingers, heavy with uncertainty: Do I ever cross your mind, or has time washed me away completely?

I hope you don't resent me or the memories we shared, though I wouldn't blame you if you did. I know I let you down—I failed you in ways a friend never should. But even so, I wish for nothing but your happiness and success. You deserve every bit of joy the world has to offer, whether I am in your life or not. And if you ever decide to reach out, I would welcome it with open arms. If life gives me the chance to be there for you again, I promise I will never repeat my mistakes.

You were one of the kindest, most loving friends I've ever had. I will forever hold that truth in my heart and continue to wish you nothing but the best.

Yours sincerely.

Reflection

This letter reflects on the painful realization of a lost friendship and the lessons it offers about cherishing those who truly care for us. It serves as a reminder to prioritize the people who stand by us, even during our moments of distraction or emotional turmoil. The key lesson here is to value the presence of those who remain steadfast in our lives and to avoid taking their kindness for granted.

If you find yourself in a similar situation, let this letter guide you to act before it's too late. Take time to nurture the relationships that matter, apologize where needed, and acknowledge the efforts of those who choose to stay. Recognizing your mistakes and growing from them not only honours the bond you shared but also shapes you into a better, more mindful friend moving forward.

Your Turn to Reflect

Key Emotions: Regret, Resentment, Reflection

Optional Prompt: Reflect on a person whose presence impacted your life profoundly but whom you regret losing. Explore the emotions tied to their absence and the gratitude or lessons their memory brings.

SNEHAL PADAYA

Dear One-Sided Love,

I've carried these feelings and thoughts within me for so long, unsure of how to bring them to light or whether they should even be shared. But they have become too heavy to hold, and it's time to let them go—even if only through the words of this letter that you may never read.

There has always been something about you that made me wonder where I truly belonged in your life. The stories you shared—of yours—the fleeting connections, tangled relationships, and endless complexities—lingered in my mind, leaving me caught in uncertainty. I wondered if I was just another fleeting presence that might eventually fade.

Was I just another passing moment, fading into the rhythm of your life? The doubt lingered, yet within me, there remains a quiet certainty—I deserve to be recognized and valued, not overshadowed. Carried by the gentle assurance that my worth is not for others to define.

And yet, I don't place all the blame on you. I, too, made choices that now leave me questioning. I stepped into moments filled with uncertainty, convincing myself they made sense—because trusting you felt less daunting than facing the doubts stirring within me.

At times, your words felt like scattered puzzle pieces—no matter how I tried, they refused to align. I searched for clarity, but the deeper I questioned, the more tangled my thoughts became. Was the truth shifting to fit your narrative, or was I merely confronting the echoes of my own uncertainties and desires? Those questions grew louder, drawing me into a cycle of unease. Perhaps my mind had already begun tracing the shape of something unspoken, sensing the weight of what lingered beneath the surface. Yet my heart resisted, caught in quiet hesitation, unwilling to surrender to what it might reveal.

By then, my thoughts had unraveled, weighed down by emotions I had quietly carried. I couldn't stop wondering if I truly mattered to you, if what we shared held meaning. You said you didn't love me romantically, and though I had known, hearing it made the truth harder to hold.

Despite everything, I want you to know how much I value the friendship we've shared. Your presence has meant so much to me, and for that, I am truly grateful. No matter what, I hope you understand that I'll always be there for you when you need me—unless your actions leave me no choice but to step away to safeguard my peace.

I wanted to open up to you, to face the uncertainty and unease—the lingering doubt of whether I was being taken for granted. Maybe I even tried, but each attempt only deepened the silence, leaving me unheard. Vulnerability wasn't something you seemed comfortable with, and eventually, I stopped reaching out—Holding onto these thoughts alone.

So here I am, writing this letter—not for you, but for me. To let these emotions—unease go, to find peace within myself, and to make sense of everything that has lingered for far too long.

It's clear to me now that what I felt for you was one-sided

love—a love tangled in confusion and longing, shaped by misaligned intentions. And yet, I hold on to the hope that fate knows what's best. Perhaps the answer lies in the very fact that I am unsure—because if it were real, I would have known without a doubt.

And so, I let go of the unease and confusion, choosing instead to honor and cherish the friendship. To believe that this chapter of complexity has fulfilled its purpose, and that I am ready to step forward with clarity and ease. If love is meant to find me, it will come—honest, unwavering, and without compromise.

Yours Truly.

Reflection

This letter captures the profound journey of one-sided love—a mix of hope, desire, doubt, and eventual clarity. It teaches an invaluable lesson about self-worth and the importance of letting go when expectation is rooted in uncertainty. By choosing to release the weight of unanswered feelings, reclaim peace, and open the door to love that is true, mutual, and fulfilling.

For readers navigating similar emotions, this reflection offers a gentle reminder: honor your feelings, but also recognize when holding on only deepens the ache. Letting go isn't surrender—it's choosing clarity over uncertainty, self-respect over waiting, and trust over fear. What is truly meant for you will come with honesty, reciprocity, and the alignment your heart deserves.

Your Turn to Reflect

Key Emotions: One-Sided Longing, Desire, Self-Worth

Optional Prompt: Reflect on a love or connection that felt one-sided. Explore the emotions tied to longing, the journey to finding closure, and the rediscovery of your worth along the way.

SNEHAL PADAYA

II

The Imprints of
Faded Wounds

In This Part

We confront the lingering ache of fractured ties—connections once vital but now worn by distance, time, misunderstandings, and unmet hopes. These letters explore the heartache of strained family bonds, broken promises, and the yearning for a closeness that feels out of reach. With honesty and vulnerability, this part echoes the lingering pain while uncovering the quiet strength that rises in its wake—transforming heartache into resilience, and healing into something beautifully unshaken.

Dear Closest Cousin,

The Brother I Hold Most Dear, I understand there was family chaos—issues that led you to distance yourself from everyone. But what about me? Wasn't I your favourite little sister, the one who admired you the most? The one who looked up to you as the most precious person in her life, someone she thought would always be there?

It broke my heart when I realized we had grown apart. As a child, I constantly asked my parents why we no longer visited your dad's place—my favourite place in the world. Their answers were always the same: "They're busy." At first, I believed them. Then, eventually, I stopped asking. As I grew older, I began to sense that something wasn't right, though I didn't know what. So, I held back and convinced myself not to push the matter.

And then, that day at the wedding happened. I saw you. After years of silence and distance, there you were, sitting across the hall. For a moment, it felt like time had rewound itself, and memories of us flooded back—the laughter, the care, the bond I thought was unbreakable. My heart swelled with emotions I couldn't fully process—joy, confusion, and an overwhelming longing. I hesitated, unsure if it was right to approach you. Would you even remember me? Or should I stay unseen, unnoticed?

And then I saw her—your wife—and your three beautiful children. Tears welled up in my eyes before I even realized it. I thought back to your first baby boy, the one I doted on so much, the one I always wanted to be there for, even though I was just a child myself. And now, there were two more children I didn't even know existed. It hit me: how much time had passed, how much I had missed, and how much I had wanted to be a part of your life all these years.

I pointed you out to Mom, my voice trembling with excitement. "Can we meet him?" I asked. But she hesitated, her smile faltering as if she already knew what I didn't. After some quiet discussion with a relative, it was decided that my uncle would speak to you first, and I would follow behind. I clung to that hope as I crossed the hall, my heart racing, tears streaming down my face, still unable to stop smiling.

When I stood behind you and heard your voice for the first time in years, I froze. My emotions overwhelmed me, and I couldn't find the courage to speak. Mom noticed and gently pulled me forward. Finally, I managed to say, "Hi, brother. How are you?" My voice wavered with hope, longing to just hug you and cry. But you ignored me.

I thought maybe you didn't recognize me. Innocently, I waited, thinking Mom's introduction would spark your memory. But even then, there was no reply. No acknowledgment. Nothing. And in that moment, my heart shattered.

I turned and ran out of the room, tears blurring everything around me. I found a corner where I let myself break down completely, crying for the brother I thought I still had. My uncle, aunt, and mom followed me, trying to console me, but their words couldn't touch the ache inside me. All I could think was, "Did he truly ignore me? Was I not as important to him as he was to me? Was I no longer his special little sister?"

On the way home, I stayed silent, trying to process what had just happened. Tears slipping down my cheeks despite my best efforts, betraying the calm mask I worked so hard to wear.

In the days that followed, I realized I needed to be strong—for myself and everyone else. I wore a brave face, smiled through the pain, and slowly began to accept that you had abandoned me, too. It hurt—more than words can ever express—but I told myself this was the answer I had been searching for all along.

So, thank you for making it clear. Thank you for teaching me, in the harshest way possible, that I needed to move on. Maybe it was a lesson in emotional strength, in learning how to grow up and guard my heart. And though it still hurts, deep down, I hold onto a sliver of hope that one day, you'll realize my absence, and decide to reconnect—not just with me, but with the whole family.

If that day ever comes, I want you to know that I would love for us to reconnect, to find a way back to the bond we once shared. But it won't be easy for me to let you back in. I've changed. I've grown into someone who values her peace, her dignity, and her emotional well-being above all else. If you ever choose to return to the family and mend what was broken. I'll need to see your effort, sincerity, and you'll need to earn back my trust—because I refuse to let myself be hurt like that again.

Still, I wish you all the happiness in the world. I hope your life with your family is as beautiful and fulfilling as you've dreamed it to be. Sending all the love I can to your wonderful children and wishing them the brightest futures. And I hope, someday, you truly understand the impact of your silence.

Yours Truly.

Reflection

This letter delves into the heartbreak of being abandoned by someone deeply cherished and the difficult process of coming to terms with the loss of that bond. It teaches an essential lesson: the importance of valuing your emotional well-being and recognizing when it's time to protect yourself from further hurt, even when it's from extended family.

For anyone navigating a similar situation, I understand it is hard to handle abandonment, especially when it is from your family member whom you were close to. The message is clear—while hope for reconciliation may remain, self-growth and boundaries must come first. Embrace your strength, guard your peace, and understand that moving on doesn't mean forgetting. It means valuing yourself enough to let go of the pain and allowing relationships to return only if they are met with sincerity and effort.

Your Turn to Reflect

Key Emotions: Abandonment, Betrayal, Resilience

• • •

Optional Prompt: Write about a moment when someone you cared for deeply became distant. Reflect on how it shaped your feelings and the strength or clarity you found in yourself as you navigated through the experience.

Dear Chosen Brother,

Some relationships are chosen—they are built on trust, shared moments, and the belief that they will endure. Ours was one of those. I chose to see you as my brother, someone I could look up to, rely on, and care for deeply. But time, misunderstandings, and silence have a way of widening even the smallest cracks, turning them into distance that feels hard to bridge.

I am writing this letter to share what's been weighing on my mind—not to blame or accuse, but to open up about the emotions I've been holding onto for so long.

Perhaps I've tried to open up before, but it never seemed to reach you in the way I hoped. I know I've made mistakes—more than a few—and I've tried to own up to them. But it often felt like those efforts weren't enough, as though the grudges you hold from the past kept pulling us back into a cycle of resentment and silence.

I don't expect forgiveness to come easily—it requires vulnerability and trust on both sides. But I've always hoped for the best and wished for you to try, at least. If forgiving me is too much, then I wish you wouldn't say that you have, only to let those same grudges linger. When old wounds turn into grudges, they create barriers that prevent relationships from moving forward.

In my own way, I was always there for you—not because I needed recognition, but because that's what mattered to me. I stood by quietly, offering support when I could, even as I started to feel the weight of compromise. Birthdays, festive days, and other moments that meant so much to me seemed to fade into the background for you. I told myself it didn't matter, that there would always be another chance, but deep down, it did matter.

I never needed to be your priority. I never wanted that. But on the rare days that truly mattered, I hoped for a sign that I mattered too. Even when I told you how I felt, you'd promise to make up for it, to make things right—but those promises often went unfulfilled. Still, I forgave, holding onto the hope that the next time might be different. Yet, as time passed, those hopes turned into quiet disappointments.

What hurt the most wasn't the missed plans or broken promises—it was the silence. When I pulled back, when I stopped answering calls, there wasn't the faintest trace that it affected you at all. When I sought resolution, it felt distant, almost indifferent, as though my absence in your life didn't make any difference. When I tried to have honest conversations, those moments often turned into reflections of the grudges you couldn't let go of, pulling us further apart.

Relationships can't survive unless both sides meet halfway. That's something I've learned over time. Even with the best intentions, no bond can flourish without effort, understanding, and care from both individuals. And while there were moments when you tried to reconnect, those attempts often felt surface-level—as if it was more about fulfilling an expectation than truly bridging the distance between us—or somehow, even when you tried, you ended up unravelling things further, making it harder to hold onto what remained.

As I prepare to leave this chapter of my life behind, I find myself holding onto the lessons this journey has taught me. I've learned the importance of protecting my peace, of letting go of the expectations that weigh us down, and of accepting that not every relationship can be what we wish it to be. Though we are growing apart, the respect and care I feel for your parents continues, and I will honour them in the ways that I can.

I hope that one day you find a way to let go of the grudges you've carried. Life is too short to live in the shadow of past hurts. Surround yourself with people who see you, who lift you, and who bring you joy.

I wish you happiness, growth, and a life filled with meaning. Wherever our paths lead, I'll hold onto the hope that one day, you'll find what you need to heal and live freely.

Yours Truly.

Reflection

This letter conveys the pain and complexity of chosen family relationships that drift apart under the weight of unresolved misunderstandings and silence. It offers an invaluable lesson: meaningful relationships require mutual effort, honesty, and a willingness to let go of past grudges to truly move forward.

For anyone in a similar situation, I understand it's hard to accept the parting when we are close to someone, that they feel like family. This reflection emphasizes the importance of protecting your peace while acknowledging the love and respect you once had for the person. It teaches that letting go of expectations allows space for healing and clarity, reminding you to prioritize connections that bring mutual care and understanding.

Your Turn to Reflect

Key Emotions: Drifting apart, Disappointment, Acceptance

Optional Prompt: Reflect on a relationship where misunderstandings and silence created distance. Explore the emotions tied to forgiveness, disappointment, or the lessons of growth you've gained from the experience.

Dear Father,

Whenever I come across videos of father-daughter bonds—those moments of laughter, connection, and shared love—I find myself scrolling past them, as if instinctively avoiding the weight they carry. They no longer feel relatable to me. Perhaps I'm shielding myself from the sadness they might bring, the emptiness of realizing those moments aren't part of my life—or haven't been for a long time.

I once came across a reel that spoke about the difference between a "father" and a "dad." It struck me deeply. Since then, even addressing you as "dad" stirs conflicting feelings, as though the word itself doesn't quite fit anymore. Writing this letter feels similar—it's difficult to put these emotions into words, and as I write, the tears come unbidden, long before I even finish a sentence.

I don't know where to begin or what to say, but there are things I must ask you: Do you notice me, truly? Do you see the loneliness I sometimes carry, even in a crowded room? Do you sense the moments when I wish for just a simple chat with you, for a chance to talk freely about anything and everything?

Do you realize that I might need you—to guide me, to protect me when I feel unsafe, to be the man I can look up to? Do you feel the distance between us, the emotional absence of your daughter in your life? Do you ever wonder what it would be like to leave the stress behind for a while, to simply spend unguarded time with family again?

Do you see the quiet wishes I don't voice anymore—like longing for even a small birthday celebration initiated by you, or a surprise gift that reminds me I'm thought of? Have you ever noticed that I hold back from saying things like, "Dad, I love this dress, this jewellery—can I have it, please?" the way a little girl might, full of innocence and trust or that I've stopped wearing jewellery for days because artificial pieces irritate my skin, and I silently dream of gold jewellery gifted by you?

Do you sense that I long to feel like your little girl again—cherished, protected, and loved, like a princess in her father's world? Do you see that I am slowly fading away from you?

Asking you these questions takes so much out of me. It pulls me into spirals of overthinking, leaving me to doubt my reality. Sometimes, I wish all of this were just a dream—a fleeting nightmare I could wake up from and leave behind forever.

Mom has told me so many stories about the person you once were—the loving husband, the devoted father. She spoke of a man who cherished his family, who found joy in the little moments, and stood unwavering through life's hardships. I wonder: if that version of you truly existed, why did it fade? I know the answer, but I still believe that even the worst circumstances can be healed, that change is possible with the right steps.

But here is the truth that hurts me the most: you haven't taken those steps. I understand the stress you're under. I've tried to stand by you, to offer my support, to see things from your perspective. But time and again, it feels as though you've chosen the same path, ignoring the chances to change. Even when those closest to you are ready to back you, you resist the right choices, keeping the walls between us intact.

I think back to our last real discussion. I gave you a choice—a chance to prove that things could be different. I made it clear that if your choices didn't change, it would be harder for me to support you. Twice, I gave you opportunities, and twice, those choices led to disappointment. Even then, I tried to stay—partially—to offer what support I could. But each time, the hurt deepened, and eventually, I began to drift away. And it didn't seem to matter to you.

Do you remember when I was little? I used to hold onto your arm everywhere we went—even when I was almost done with school—because it made me feel safe. I remember the day you told me I was too old to do that anymore, that none of your friends' daughters clung to their fathers like that. It made me sad, but I held my ground and said firmly, "So what? Are your friends influencing you negatively?" Not long after, one day, you smiled and told me that your friends praised how close we were, how I still held your arm. Those memories feel distant now, part of a version of us that's hard to recognize.

Now, when you speak to me, it often feels functional—like you're asking for something, not seeking a real conversation. We don't have casual chats anymore, no moments of shared connection. I question your words, wondering if there's always something you need behind them.

Despite everything, I've always wanted to be there for you. I still worry about you and hope you're okay. But remember, it's because of you that I've started to fade away.

I hope you choose better—for yourself, for your health, for the family that still cares for you. I hope you find the strength to take those steps, to become the person Mom describes so fondly. She still hopes for that version of you, and perhaps, so do I.

Yours Truly.

Reflection

This letter expresses the profound yearning for connection and closeness with a distant parent, offering a heartfelt expression of the emotional gap that can grow over time.

For readers who find themselves in a similar situation, this reflection encourages honest introspection. It highlights the need to acknowledge the pain of disconnection while also recognizing the strength it takes to hope for change. The absence of emotional warmth from a parent can be one of the most difficult lessons for a child to grasp—not only because love is absent, but also because it is expressed in ways that feel unfamiliar or unreachable. Understanding emotional distance requires patience, self-compassion, and the ability to differentiate between absence and silence, so take your time and heal, as you don't deserve to dwell in it.

Your Turn to Reflect

Key Emotions: Distant Parent, Emotional Unavailability, Loneliness

Optional Prompt: Reflect on a relationship that feels distant or emotionally absent. Explore the feelings of longing, the hope for change, or the possibility of reconnecting and rebuilding the bond.

• 50 •

HEALING AS I WRITE

III

Choosing Peace & Growth

In This Part

We embrace the courage to let go and honor the paths that lead to inner peace. Through letters of forgiveness, self-reflection, and wisdom, this part celebrates the resilience forged through overcoming challenges. These reflections invite you to release the weight of the past, rediscover your strength, and move forward with clarity and compassion.

Dear You,

All Those I am Forgiving, there was a time when your words, your actions, and your silence cut deep. A time when I replayed everything—every disappointment, every wound—as though dissecting the pain might make it hurt less. But it never did.

Forgiveness was never about erasing what happened or pretending that the pain didn't shape me. I used to believe that forgiving meant giving up my right to feel hurt, that it meant losing power over the situation. But I've come to learn that forgiveness is not about surrendering—it's about reclaiming. It is a choice to rise above resentment and take back control of my heart, my peace, and my life.

To the friend who turned their back on me when I needed them most: I forgive you—not because you asked for it, but because your absence will no longer dictate my ability to trust others.

To the loved one whose silence broke me when they should have held me together: I forgive you—not because your silence wasn't hurtful, but because I refuse to be defined by the hurt they left behind.

To those whose actions wounded me in ways they may never fully understand: I forgive you—not because the act itself was forgivable, but because I deserve the freedom of letting it go.

And to the people I've held in my thoughts for so long—those whose influence has shaped the way I love, the way I protect myself, and the way I move forward: I forgive you—not because it erases the lessons learned, but because releasing anger allows me to grow.

Forgiveness does not mean forgetting. I will never forget the impact of what happened or the lessons it brought. They remain etched into my heart, shaping the way I guard myself, the way I trust, and the way I find strength in vulnerability. But I am done carrying bitterness, anger, and the hope for apologies that may never come.

I forgive you—not because you have earned it, but because I deserve peace. I forgive you because holding onto anger suffocates what matters most in life. I forgive you because healing begins when I choose myself over the pain of the past.

Closure no longer depends on you—I've found it within myself. And that is enough.

With quiet strength,

Me.

Reflection

This letter embodies the transformative power of forgiveness—not as an act of absolution for others, but as a profound way to reclaim your peace and emotional freedom. It teaches that forgiveness is not about erasing the pain or forgetting the lessons learned, but about releasing the grip of resentment that holds you back.

For anyone grappling with anger or hurt, this reflection serves as a reminder: forgiveness is a gift you give yourself, allowing you to move forward without the weight of bitterness. It empowers you to find closure within, independent of apologies or external validation. The act of forgiving is a step toward healing, growth, and embracing a life guided by inner peace and strength.

Your Turn to Reflect

Key Emotions: Forgiveness, Empowerment, Reassurance

Optional Prompt: Reflect on a moment when you found the strength to forgive someone—not for their sake, but for your own. Explore how forgiveness helped you reclaim your peace and begin the journey toward healing.

Dear Me,

There was a time when I believed the weight of disappointment, heartbreak, and lost connections would crush me entirely. I carried them like invisible chains, feeling every rejection, every failure, every silence as a defining blow. For so long, I thought those moments of pain were permanent scars, an inescapable part of me. But here I am—still standing, breathing, and moving forward.

I have survived the days of feeling abandoned, when no one reached out, when silence echoed louder than words. I have endured the heartbreak of waiting for promises to be fulfilled, only for the world to leave me unanswered. I have lived through the nights of doubting my worth, wondering if I was enough. I have felt the ache of friendships lost, the sting of realizing that some people will never love me the way I love them—and that some connections fade no matter how tightly you hold onto them.

And yet, I rise. Not because someone rescued me, not because life magically became easier, but because I found something within myself that was stronger than the pain. I discovered that I am enough—more than enough. Through solitude, I found resilience. Through heartbreak, I found wisdom. Through vulnerability, I uncovered courage.

I have walked through storms that seemed relentless, storms that tried to drown me in their fury. But what I discovered was far greater than survival: I am the storm itself. I am capable of rebuilding, reshaping, and standing stronger than ever before. When the world tried to bury me, I learned how to rise.

I am not a victim of my past. I am not defined by the people who walked away or the choices I made in moments of weakness. I am becoming—and that is a journey worth celebrating. Growth is not linear, and healing is never perfect, but each step forward is proof of my strength, of my will to create a life of meaning and joy.

To anyone who faces similar moments of despair, I offer this: You are stronger than you believe. The weight you carry may feel unbearable now, but it does not define you. You are more than the mistakes made against you or the wounds inflicted by others. Even in your darkest hours, even when you question your place in the world, remember this: You are worthy of love, of healing, and joy.

You don't need permission to let go of resentment and anger—they are chains that serve no purpose. Forgiving yourself, forgiving others, doesn't mean forgetting or condoning what happened; it means choosing freedom. Freedom to live without carrying that weight, freedom to rebuild yourself for the future you deserve.

To myself, I say this with unwavering clarity: The hard days will come again, but I know now that I am prepared to face them. Life will test me, but I will not let it break me. I am my own anchor, my own light, and my own storm. I rise not despite the pain, but because of it.

And above all else, I love you. I love the strength that has carried you through storms, the courage that has rebuilt you time and time again, the heart that refuses to give up hope. I promise to never let you down, to never stop believing in your worth, to never stop loving who you are and who you are becoming. You are enough, and you always will be.

With unwavering strength and infinite hope,

Me.

Reflection

This letter is a powerful testament to resilience and self-love, reminding us that even in our darkest moments, we hold the strength to rise and rebuild. It teaches the invaluable lesson that pain does not define us—it shapes us, but the choice to heal and grow is ours alone.

For readers who may feel weighed down by struggles or self-doubt, this reflection offers guidance: trust in your ability to overcome challenges, embrace the journey of becoming, and choose freedom by letting go of resentment and anger. You are more than your past, and each step toward healing is a step toward joy, strength, and self-acceptance. Let this reflection inspire you to honor your worth and rise—not despite the pain, but because of it.

Your Turn to Reflect

Key Emotions: Resilience, Self-Love, Growth

Optional Prompt: Reflect on a moment when you found inner strength to overcome a challenge. Write about how embracing self-love and resilience shaped your healing journey. You may also write a heartfelt letter to yourself, offering encouragement, hope, and acknowledgment of how far you've come.

Dear Strength,

You have always been there, quietly waiting for me to see you—to acknowledge your presence within me. You didn't shout for attention or demand recognition; instead, you revealed yourself in the moments I least expected, when life tested me in ways I feared I couldn't endure.

When the weight of the world bore down on me, I doubted myself. I questioned my ability to rise above the storms. But you showed up, steady and unwavering, carrying me through each wave. You weren't loud or dramatic; you were persistent, guiding me to keep moving forward, even when my steps felt heavy.

Strength, I see you now, not just in the victories but in the struggles themselves. You appeared in the cracks where I thought I'd broken, reminding me that those cracks didn't shatter me—they shaped me. They revealed the light within, the resilience I didn't realize was mine all along.

You taught me that strength isn't about being unshaken—it's about moving forward despite the fear, despite the pain, despite the uncertainty. You weren't a gift handed to me by someone else; you were a truth I earned, a part of me I discovered through every challenge I faced.

To anyone reading this: Strength doesn't always feel heroic. It's not always bold or brash. Sometimes, it's the quiet determination to keep going when it feels impossible. It's the choice to believe in yourself even when the world seems to be against you. Strength is in the endurance, the courage, the simple act of carrying on.

Thank you, Strength, for teaching me what I'm capable of—not in spite of the storms but because of them. You've been my guide, my shield, my reason to rise again. Knowing that the strength we are looking for is within ourselves is invaluable.

With gratitude,

Me.

Reflection

Strength isn't about always being confident or unshaken—it's about the quiet persistence that carries us forward, even in the face of fear and doubt. It hides in the moments we rise after falling and in the determination we show when we keep going despite adversity. Recognizing your strength is a way to honor the resilience you've cultivated through life's challenges. It's not a gift given to you—it's a force you've discovered within yourself.

Your Turn to Reflect

Key Emotion: Strength, Determination, Self-empowerment

Optional Prompt: Write a letter to your strength, thanking it for being the foundation of your growth and recognising it.

Dear Me,

There are so many things you've carried for far too long—moments you wish you could rewrite, words you wish you hadn't said, decisions you regret with all your heart. You've held these things so tightly, as if clinging to them could somehow make up for them. As if punishing yourself for your mistakes could undo them, heal the wounds, or erase the past. But it doesn't work that way, does it?

You've blamed yourself when you should have understood. You've judged yourself when you should have been kind. You've whispered words of self-criticism when what you needed most was reassurance. And through it all, you've forgotten something so simple, so vital: You're human.

Humans make mistakes. We falter, we fail, we hurt others—sometimes even ourselves. But those mistakes are not the end of the story. They do not define you. They do not erase the goodness in you, the effort you've made, the love you've given, the strength you've shown.

So, let's start here, with the words you've needed to hear all along: I forgive you.

I forgive you for the decisions made in fear, for the words spoken in anger, for the moments when you didn't know any better. I forgive you for holding onto guilt that isn't yours to carry and for placing blame where it doesn't belong. I forgive you for being imperfect—for being human.

It's time to let go. Not of the lessons, because there is

wisdom in your experiences, but of the weight. It's time to stop asking yourself to be flawless and start asking yourself to be kind. To offer the same compassion to yourself that you so easily give to others.

You've been so strong for so long, even when it felt impossible. You've done your best, even when you thought it wasn't enough. And now, it's time to let yourself breathe. To remember that you're worthy—not because of perfection, but because of the effort, the resilience, the hope that keeps you moving forward.

Forgiveness doesn't mean forgetting. It means choosing to move forward without carrying the burden of the past. And you deserve that freedom.

So, dear me, here's to releasing the weight. Here's to embracing the messy, beautiful journey of being human. Here's to you—worthy, imperfect, and deserving of love, just as you are.

I love you a lot and will always keep loving you, so be gentle with yourself.

Always yours,

Me.

Reflection

Self-forgiveness is not about forgetting your mistakes—it's about releasing the guilt that keeps you from growing. It's about recognizing your humanity and choosing kindness over judgment.

It can be difficult to forgive yourself, but it's one of the most powerful steps toward healing. When you let go of self-blame, you open the door to self-compassion, growth, and peace.

Remember: self-forgiveness is not an act of weakness; it's an act of courage and strength.

Guidance for Forgiving Yourself:

- Reflect on the mistakes that weigh you down and what you've learned from them.
- Acknowledge your humanity—imperfection is a shared experience, not a flaw.
- Compassion over judgment—replace blame with understanding.

Your Turn to Reflect

Key emotions: Self-blame, Self-compassion, Kindness

Optional prompt: What is one mistake or regret that you've struggled to forgive yourself for? How can you rewrite your story to recognize the lessons and forgive yourself?

Dear Shame,

You've been a quiet yet persistent companion, weaving yourself into the fabric of my thoughts. You don't knock or announce your arrival—you simply appear, uninvited. Sometimes you take the form of regret, lingering over a choice I can't undo. Other times, you creep into my reflection, turning my gaze toward imperfections I was taught to hide. And then there are moments you whisper, telling me I've fallen short—in their eyes, in mine.

You've worn many faces: the guilt of past actions, the discomfort of imperfection, the ache of failing to meet expectations. I carried you, mistaking your weight for something I was supposed to bear. You convinced me I had to, that your presence was proof of my flaws, my failures, my inadequacies. For so long, I believed you.

But I see you now, Shame. You are not my truth; you are a voice born of fear and doubt. You thrive in silence, growing stronger in the spaces where I hide. You made me believe that every mistake was irreparable, every imperfection unlovable, every failure final. You led me to question my worth, my belonging, my very humanity.

Yet, here I stand—writing to you, reclaiming the space you've stolen. My mistakes do not define me; they teach me. My body does not need your approval; it carries me, and that is enough. My worth is not something you get to measure—it is inherent, simply because I exist, because I try, because I grow.

To the ones reading these words: if you feel the weight of

shame pressing on your heart, know this—shame does not define you. It thrives on the lies it tells, but the truth is far greater. You are enough, just as you are. Flawed, imperfect, and human—and within that humanity lies your beauty. Whatever your story, keep finding your strength, keep moving forward, and just keep improving.

Goodbye, Shame. You no longer have a place here. Let this serve as a firm reminder that even if you return, your hold over me will never be the same. You will not drag me down again. I will observe and improve.

No longer yours,

Me.

Reflection

Shame often emerges uninvited, weaving into our thoughts and shaping the way we see ourselves. It convinces us that our mistakes define us, that our imperfections must be hidden, and that we are unworthy of love or acceptance. But shame is built on distortions—it thrives in silence, gaining strength from the stories it tells us about who we are.

Healing begins by recognizing shame for what it truly is: a voice of fear and self-doubt, not truth. To confront it is to reclaim the parts of yourself that shame has tried to take away—your confidence, your humanity, your inherent worth. It's about letting your flaws and struggles be a testament to your growth, not a reason to hide.

Releasing shame takes time, but every act of self-compassion is a step forward. As you choose truth over doubt, you embrace the freedom that comes from knowing you are enough, just as you are.

Your Turn to Reflect

Key emotions: Shame, Self-compassion, Realisation

• 79 •

Optional prompt: What part of yourself have you hidden because of shame's whispers? How can you reclaim it and rewrite the story that honors your worth?

Dear Younger Me,

I can see you now—standing in the middle of those carefree days, when life feels so simple and full of possibilities. Your laughter fills the air, unrestrained, as you find joy in the small moments that make everything feel light and easy. There's an innocence in the way you embrace life, trusting the world and the people in it with all your heart. These are the moments to treasure, the days that remind you of just how beautiful and vibrant life can be.

But as life moves forward, you are starting to notice some things shift—and not fully understanding why. There's a growing unease, a quiet uncertainty that begins to sneak into your thoughts. You start feeling emotions you can't quite name or explain—like sadness, restlessness, or even frustration—and they swirl together in ways that catch you off guard. You wonder why you're feeling these things and what they mean, and this uncertainty might start to feel overwhelming.

And that's okay. Those feelings, as unexpected and unsettling as they seem, are not here to defeat you. They're here to guide you. They're here to remind you that growth comes from moments of discomfort, and that uncertainty is not something to fear—it's a sign that you're discovering yourself, piece by piece, and becoming the person you're meant to be.

However, it's just as important to understand when to pause and protect yourself. There will be times when something feels wrong—a conversation, a situation, or even a relationship. Listen to that instinct. It's your inner voice trying to shield you, to draw boundaries where they are needed. Knowing when to stop, to step back, or to say "no" is an act of self-love, not weakness. Pay attention to how you feel, and don't be afraid to put yourself first when something threatens your peace. Walking away when necessary isn't giving up—it's safeguarding the person you're becoming.

Your emotions might feel confusing and heavy at times, but they are not your enemies. They are your teachers, here to show you what matters, where your boundaries lie, and what your heart truly desires. Let me share what I've come to understand about these feelings:

- **Anger** reveals where your boundaries have been crossed—it teaches you to protect what's important.
- **Jealousy** shines a light on your aspirations—it guides you toward what you truly want.
- **Shame** uncovers the parts of you that need healing and self-compassion.
- **Anxiety** asks you to build trust and confidence—it invites you to face uncertainty with courage.
- **Fear** shows you the path to your greatest growth—it's where your strength is waiting to be uncovered.

These emotions are not weaknesses; they are signs of your resilience and your capacity to feel deeply. They're not here to break you; they're here to guide you.

When those emotions feel too heavy, remember to pause and care for yourself. Find small, grounding acts that remind you of your own power:

- **When you feel like you hate everyone**: Eat something nourishing—it will bring you comfort.
- **When you feel like everyone hates you**: Rest and sleep—it will reset your mind and soothe your heart.
- **When you feel like you hate yourself**: Take a shower—let the water refresh and calm you.
- **When your thoughts feel overwhelming**: Write them down—let them flow out and clear your mind.
- **When you feel stuck in the past**: Plan for the future—remind yourself of what's yet to come.
- **When you feel anxious about the future**: Anchor yourself in the present—focus on what you can do right now.
- **When you feel restless**: Take a walk—let the rhythm of your steps bring clarity.
- **When you feel like giving up**: Remember a time when you triumphed—let that memory remind you of your resilience.

You don't need to have all the answers right now. Life isn't about being perfect; it's about learning, growing, and finding your way. Each moment of sadness or uncertainty will teach you something important, something that will shape the person you are becoming.

Dear younger me, you are stronger than you know. You are worthy of love, respect, and happiness—not because of what you accomplish, but simply because of who you are. Even when the world feels heavy, even when doubt creeps in, I want you to hold onto this truth: You are enough. Exactly as you are.

And above all, I want you to know this: I love you. I love

your heart, your courage, and your determination to keep moving forward, no matter what. I promise I will never let you down. I will always believe in you. You are more than capable of facing whatever comes your way—and you are worth it, always.

With endless love and unwavering faith,

Me.

Reflection

This letter is a heartfelt guide to navigating life's emotional highs and lows, reminding us of the transformative power of self-awareness, resilience, and self-love. It teaches the essential lesson that emotions, even the heavy ones, are not weaknesses but valuable teachers guiding us toward personal growth and strength.

For readers, the takeaway is twofold: honor your feelings and never let them go unaddressed. Ignoring emotions or bottling them up can lead to overwhelming moments when they eventually surface. Recognizing and expressing them, whether through reflection, conversation, or self-care, prevents this buildup and fosters clarity, healing, and inner peace. This letter encourages you to trust your instincts, embrace vulnerability, and prioritize self-care as a vital act of love for yourself. Let it remind you that you are worthy of growth, happiness, and above all, the freedom to thrive.

Your Turn to Reflect

Key Emotions: Self-Awareness, Growth, Self-Love

Optional Prompt: Write a letter to your younger self, offering encouragement and understanding. Reflect on the emotions that shaped you and the lessons you've learned on your journey of healing and growth. Embrace the resilience and love that continue to guide you forward.

IV

Embracing Hope & Moving Forward

In This Part

We step into the light of hope and possibility, embracing the quiet resilience that carries us forward. These letters explore growth, trust, and the profound strength that comes from surrendering to the unseen powers that guide us. This part celebrates the beauty of embracing the unknown with faith, optimism, and an open heart toward what's yet to come.

Dear Future Me,

I wonder what your days look like now. Have you created the life you once dreamed of, or have your dreams evolved into something even greater, something unexpected? Wherever you are, I hope you're waking up with purpose and resting your head at night with peace. But most of all, I hope you've become someone you're proud of—not because of what you've achieved, but because of who you are.

As I write to you, I'm sitting here with all the questions that fill the gap between now and where you are. I know the road ahead won't always be smooth. Life has a way of throwing us into storms we never anticipated. But I hope you've learned to see the storms for what they are—temporary. I hope you've found the strength to weather them, to walk through the rain without losing your belief in the sun.

I know there will be moments when you've felt like giving up, when the weight of uncertainty made every step forward feel impossible. But if you're reading this, then you didn't give up. You kept moving. You found reasons—tiny, quiet reasons—to keep believing, to keep trying. For that, I'm already so proud of you.

Have you learned how to listen to your own voice—the one that so often gets drowned out by the noise of the world? Have you stopped apologizing for who you are or shrinking yourself to fit into spaces that were never meant for you? I hope you've learned to stand tall in your truth, no matter how uncomfortable it makes others.

I hope you've let go of the things that were never yours to carry—the burdens of resentment, fear, and the expectations of others. I hope you've made peace with the chapters of life that didn't go the way you'd hoped, and I hope you've found the courage to begin again, over and over, whenever it was necessary.

Please tell me you've held on to the things that matter: the people who make you laugh even when life feels heavy, the moments that fill your heart instead of your schedule, the dreams that scare you because they mean so much. I hope you've embraced joy—not as a luxury, but as a birthright.

And when it comes to love, I hope you've stopped chasing perfection. I hope you've realized that love doesn't need to be grand or flawless to be real. The truest love, whether it's for yourself, your dreams, or another person, is found in the messy, unfiltered moments of life.

If you're looking back at me right now, I want you to know I'm doing my best to lay the foundation for you. I'm not perfect—I stumble, I second-guess, I get scared—but I'm building something I hope you'll be proud to stand on.

So, future me, wherever you are: I love you. I love the scars you've earned and the lessons you've learned. I love the bravery it took to get here. I love the mistakes that shaped you and the victories that reminded you of your strength.

Don't forget that life will continue to change in ways we can't predict. The person you are today is not the person you will be tomorrow, and that's a beautiful thing. Keep evolving. Keep growing. Keep finding new ways to love the life you're living.

With all the hope and faith I have,

Me.

Reflection

This letter celebrates the journey of growth, resilience, and self-discovery, offering hope and encouragement to embrace the unpredictability of life. It teaches a vital lesson: progress is not about perfection but about perseverance, self-love, and the courage to evolve beyond fear and doubt.

For readers, the message is both grounding and empowering—recognize that life's storms are temporary and that each challenge shapes you into someone stronger and wiser. Listen to your inner voice, let go of burdens that do not serve you, and cherish the moments and people that truly matter. The letter reminds us to trust the process, honor our imperfections, and embrace the beautiful, messy journey of becoming who we're meant to be. You are enough, and each step forward is a testament to your strength.

Your Turn to Reflect

Key Emotions: Vision, Resilience, Self-Discovery

• 94 •

Optional Prompt: Imagine writing a letter to your future self. Reflect on the dreams you hope to achieve, the challenges you might overcome, and the person you aspire to be. Celebrate the lessons you've learned and the strength that guides you toward healing and growth.

• 95 •

Dear Hope,

There were days when I doubted you were real. Days when you felt like nothing more than a comforting myth—a word people clung to for solace. You seemed distant, an unreachable promise, especially when the weight of the world made everything feel impossible. Yet, even in those darkest moments, you never abandoned me.

You were there, quietly persistent, even when I failed to recognize you. You lingered in the soft light of mornings, where the sun rose regardless of how heavy my heart felt. You whispered in unexpected places: in the laughter of strangers, in melodies that made me feel seen, and in stories that reminded me I wasn't alone.

You never demanded my attention, never shouted to be heard. Instead, you waited—patient and steadfast—for me to notice you. You stayed with me when I couldn't stay with myself, offering the faintest glimmers of belief when I had none.

Now, I see you in everything. I see you in the way time gently softens even the sharpest edges of pain. I see you in the way wounds close, the way hearts mend, and the way people find their way back to themselves. You are there in my dreams, in my small, quiet efforts, and in my choice to keep loving, even when love has been accompanied by loss.

You are resilience in its most tender form—a quiet strength that doesn't need to prove itself. You are the reason I keep moving forward, the reason I still try, the reason I dare to believe in the possibilities ahead.

For all the times I thought I had lost you, for all the times you carried me when I couldn't carry myself, I thank you. You are not just an idea—I see now that you are the essence of everything I am and everything I can be.

With gratitude,

Me.

Reflection

This letter beautifully captures the quiet yet unwavering presence of hope, even in the darkest moments of life. It teaches us that hope isn't loud or demanding; it's a gentle, persistent force that guides us when all else feels lost. The lesson here is to trust in its subtle strength, to see hope not as a fleeting feeling but as resilience in its purest form.

For readers, the message is clear: even when hope feels distant, it lingers in the smallest of moments—the sunrise, a kind word, or a simple act of love. By acknowledging its presence, even in the hardest times, you empower yourself to move forward with faith in the possibilities ahead. Let this letter remind you that hope is not just something to hold onto; it's a part of who you are, quietly driving you toward healing and renewal.

Your Turn to Reflect

Key Emotions: Hope, Resilience, Renewal

• • •

Optional Prompt: Write about a time when hope felt distant, yet quietly guided you forward. Reflect on how it helped you heal, rebuild, or find strength in small moments. You can also write a letter to hope itself, expressing your gratitude and how it shapes your journey.

Dear Universe,

There have been moments when I felt surrounded by silence so heavy it almost spoke. Moments when friendships faded like distant echoes, when the people I leaned on felt out of reach, and I was convinced I was utterly alone. The weight of those days stayed with me, and yet—somehow—I kept moving. Somehow, even when my heart was broken, even when I thought I couldn't take another step forward, the world kept turning. And so did I.

Was it you? Were you there, watching quietly as I stumbled my way through the chaos? Were you the one shifting the threads I couldn't see, nudging me forward when I wanted to stop? I've questioned you, doubted you, even argued with you. There have been days when I begged you for answers and nights when I wondered if you were there at all. But now I understand something I couldn't before: even when I didn't see you, even when I doubted, you stayed.

I used to ask you for certainty—desperately searching for meaning in the mess, for clarity that never seemed to come. But now I see that your answers were never meant to be simple or direct. You gave me experiences instead—moments that shaped me, lessons I didn't know I needed, and choices that taught me more than words ever could. You let me falter so I could learn to stand again. You gave me space to grow in ways I never expected.

Thank you for the blessings that disguised themselves as challenges, for the redirections that saved me from paths I wasn't meant to follow, and for the healing that arrived in quiet moments when I thought all was lost. Thank you for the clarity that came not in answers, but in time—the kind of clarity that reveals itself softly, like the first light of dawn.

I might not always understand your ways. In fact, there are times when your plans leave me confused, questioning, and even frustrated. But I am learning to trust you—not blindly, but with the knowledge that you move in ways I may never fully grasp. Whether you're the Universe, Almighty, God, or the Unseen Forces that shape this life, I want to thank you. Thank you for guiding me, even when I wasn't ready to listen.

So here's my promise to you: I'll keep listening to your quiet whispers. I'll keep trusting that even in the mess, there is meaning waiting to be found. I'll keep moving forward, step by step, even when the path feels uncertain.

With gratitude,

Me.

Reflection

This letter speaks to the quiet, often unseen forces that guide us through life's challenges and uncertainties. It teaches an invaluable lesson: clarity and growth rarely come from direct answers but through experiences that shape us in profound ways. Even in moments of doubt, the Universe—or what one believes in—continues to guide, support, and teach.

For readers, the takeaway is to trust the process, even when life feels chaotic or unclear. Embrace the lessons disguised as challenges and the redirections that protect you from paths not meant for you. This letter inspires gratitude for unseen guidance, patience in the face of confusion, and the courage to keep moving forward with faith in the journey ahead. Trust that meaning will reveal itself in time, just as the first light breaks through the darkest night.

Your Turn to Reflect

Key Emotions: Trust, Spirituality, Upliftment

Optional Prompt: Reflect on how the challenges in life have shaped your journey of healing and growth. Write about the moments when unseen forces—or your own resilience—guided you forward, even through uncertainty. You may also write a letter to the Universe, god or energy you believe in, expressing trust and gratitude for the lessons and clarity it has offered.

Dear Life,

Thank you—for everything. For the moments that lifted me and the moments that broke me. For the gifts that came wrapped in joy and the lessons disguised in pain. You've given me more than I could have ever asked for, though often not in the way I expected.

There were days when I doubted you, questioned your fairness, and felt burdened by your weight. Yet, through every challenge, you showed me a side of myself I hadn't known before. You taught me resilience when I thought I was weak. You gave me wisdom in the aftermath of struggle. You helped me see beauty even in the messiest of moments.

In the quietness of the everyday, you've gifted me small joys—a warm sunrise, a familiar laugh, the comfort of being understood. These moments remind me of your endless grace and the richness of simply being here. Even when you've been unpredictable, even when your lessons were hard-earned, you've shaped me into someone who sees the value in it all.

To anyone reading this: Life will challenge you. It will push you, test you, and, at times, feel unbearably heavy. But it will also lift you. It will open your heart to love, your mind to possibility, and your spirit to growth. Gratitude doesn't ignore the hard moments; it finds meaning in them and celebrates the strength you've gained along the way.

Thank you, Life, for being imperfect yet beautiful, challenging yet rewarding. You've given me more than I could have imagined, and for that, I am deeply grateful.

Sincerely,

Me.

Reflection

Gratitude is a powerful lens through which we view life. It doesn't deny the hardships we've faced but reframes them, revealing the lessons and growth hidden within. Every struggle carries wisdom, and every moment of joy reminds us that life, though imperfect, is beautiful. Practicing gratitude allows us to embrace life in its entirety—the good, the challenging, and the in-between—with an open heart.

Your Turn to Reflect

Key Emotion: Blessed, Reflection, Acceptance

•

Optional Prompt: Identify three things, big or small, that you feel grateful for today or write a letter to life, expressing appreciation for its lessons and joys, both bitter and sweet.

BEYOND THE LETTERS

Express, Heal, Manifest: The Energy Of Your Words

Healing is not just found in the words we write—it is awakened through the **act of writing itself**. Words hold energy. Every unspoken thought, every emotion left unexpressed, settles within us, shaping our experiences in ways we often don't recognize. This is why **expression is healing**—when we voice our truths, whether on paper or aloud, we unlock space for growth, release, and transformation.

Manifestation Through Frequency &
Vibrations

Everything in the universe operates on vibrations and frequencies—including our thoughts, emotions, and words. The energy we emit through self-expression and affirmation influences the reality we create.

✦ High-frequency emotions like gratitude, love, and clarity attract abundance and healing.
✦ Low-frequency emotions like fear, doubt, and guilt often manifest as resistance and stagnation.

When we write down our thoughts, affirmations, and desires, we align ourselves with the energy we want to embody. Journaling shifts stagnant emotions, allowing our frequency to rise and synchronize with our deepest intentions.

Journaling Prompts for Healing & Vibrational Alignment

To help you elevate your personal frequency and intentionally reshape your energy, you can use these guided journaling prompts mentioned below, Journaling is the act of writing down thoughts, emotions, and experiences as a way to reflect, heal, and gain clarity whereas, Affirmations are positive, intentional statements that help shift one's mindset and frequency toward growth, confidence, and manifestation.

Self-Reflection & Frequency Awareness

- How do my current emotions affect my vibrational frequency?
- What limiting beliefs keep me stuck in low-energy patterns, and how can I release them?
- What practices make me feel light, energized, and free?

Personal Growth & Alignment

- Write a letter to your future self, describing the life you are manifesting.
- What energy do I radiate in different situations, and how can I shift it positively?
- List three small daily actions that will help raise my frequency.

Manifestation & Affirmation Power

- How can I use affirmations to reshape my reality and elevate my mindset?
- Write five high-frequency affirmations that align with your most powerful self.
- What would happen if I lived as if my manifestations were already reality?

Frequency Affirmations to Elevate Your Energy

Suggestion to reinforce high-frequency vibrations:
Repeat these powerful affirmations aloud or write them down:

"I am a magnet for healing, abundance, and growth."
"My words and thoughts shape my reality with clarity and confidence."
"I release what lowers my energy, and I welcome what uplifts me."
"Every emotion I express clears space for transformation and manifestation."

Words carry energy, and your voice is a force of creation. Through journaling, intentional writing, and affirmations, you are not just reflecting—you are shifting, healing, and manifesting the life that aligns with your highest frequency.

To My Readers

Dear readers,

As I write this to you, I'm overwhelmed by gratitude. Thank you for choosing to open these pages, for allowing my words to touch your journey, and for connecting with the reflections, emotions, and lessons within. You are the soul of this book, breathing life into its letters with your unique experiences and perspectives.

This book was never intended to be just a collection of letters—it is a bridge between my heart and yours. Each word holds an invitation for you to pause, to feel, to reflect. These letters are not just my stories; they are spaces where you can find pieces of your own. They are whispers of courage, a hand to hold in moments of doubt, and an embrace in times when you need to feel less alone.

But this, dear reader, is only the beginning. If there's one wish I have for you, it is this: Write your own letters. Let these pages inspire you to unearth the emotions you may have tucked away, to release the unspoken words, and to speak to the parts of yourself that long to be heard. Whether your letters are to someone you've lost, someone you've loved, or to yourself, writing is a gift you give to your soul. It allows you to confront, to release, and ultimately to heal.

I also want you to remember this truth, one that is universal and unshakable: You are enough, just as you are. Life may not have always been kind, and the road ahead may still hold challenges, but within you is a strength you may not yet have fully recognized. You carry the power to heal, to grow, to love, and to dream. You are capable of creating a life that resonates with joy and purpose, no matter what your past has held.

As you reach the final pages of this book, know that my words are simply a companion to yours. Keep writing. Keep reflecting. Keep growing into the person you are meant to be. I hope this book has been more than a collection of letters—I hope it has been a reminder of your worth, your resilience, and the infinite possibilities that lie before you.

From the depths of my heart, thank you for sharing this journey with me. Your story matters. Your voice matters. And I believe in the extraordinary path that lies ahead of you.

With endless gratitude and love,

Snehal.

As we turn the final page of this book, I want to leave you with one last thought—a reflection on the journey we've shared and the one that lies ahead of you. These letters were never meant to provide perfect answers, but rather to guide you to moments of understanding, of courage, and of growth. They were a window into emotions we all experience, an invitation to confront, embrace, and rise above the challenges that shape us.

Life is not a single, linear story. It's a mosaic made of triumphs, heartbreaks, lessons, and moments of joy. I hope that through these letters, you've found a piece of your own journey reflected back at you—a spark of hope, a reminder of your resilience, or the courage to write your next chapter with intention.

But this isn't the end. It is merely a pause—a moment to breathe, to reflect, and to gather your strength. Moving forward, I encourage you to carry what you've learned here into the world. Nurture the relationships that uplift you, set boundaries where they're needed, and never stop believing in your ability to grow. Trust that even in the messiness of life, there is beauty waiting to be found.

Thank you for allowing me to share this journey with you. You've gifted these words with meaning by bringing your own emotions, experiences, and reflections to them. Now, as you step into the next chapter of your life, remember that you are enough, just as you are. Keep dreaming boldly, loving fiercely, and moving forward with the quiet confidence of someone who knows their worth, becoming your best version.

Wherever life takes you, may you rise to greater heights and embrace the endless possibilities ahead.

With all my love and hope for your journey,

Snehal.

FROM ME TO YOU—A GENTLE REMINDER YOU CAN'T IGNORE

Hey, you. Yes, YOU, the one reading this.

I know you've felt emotions—maybe the very ones in this book, maybe even more intense, or in ways only you truly understand. Some come and go, light and fleeting. Others settle deep, demanding to be acknowledged, refusing to stay buried.

As your well-wisher, I don't just want to remind you—**I want to warn you:**
<u>Never, ever ignore what you feel.</u> No matter how unfamiliar, inconvenient, or seemingly insignificant they may feel. Every emotion has a reason for being there. Even the ones that confuse you. Even the ones you wish would simply disappear by themselves.

Think of your emotions as a lifelong friend. Some days, they bring warmth, comfort, and joy. Other days, they test your patience, unpredictable and overwhelming. But like any true friend, they don't ask for perfection—they just ask to be heard.

So <u>sit</u> with them. <u>Acknowledge</u> them. <u>Listen</u>. And <u>try to understand</u> what they are telling you. If there's something you can do to respond to a feeling, do it. If there's nothing to change, then simply recognize that it's okay to feel the way you do—and instead of resisting, embrace your emotions with kindness.

I know exactly what you're thinking—"Easier said than done." Or maybe, "Sure, but does this really work?" Or even, "Emotions as friends? That's a bit much." And of course, "Sit with them? How do you even do that?"

But trust me, I had the same doubts when my counselor first said that to me. I remember sitting there, tangled in questions—Why am I feeling this way? How do I handle it? Does it even matter? It was frustrating, like grasping at something invisible, trying to hold onto something I didn't yet understand.

Then, my counselor told me something that changed everything. She said, "Emotions don't vanish when ignored. They gather, layer by layer, until one day, they erupt—unexpected, overwhelming, impossible to contain." Like a volcano—silent for years, seemingly harmless—until suddenly, without warning, it explodes.

And in that moment, I understood. Avoiding emotions doesn't erase them. It only makes them louder, waiting for the right time to break free.

So remember, your emotions aren't obstacles to overcome. They are parts of you—real, raw, and necessary. The more space you give them, the more you will understand yourself. And maybe, they'll lead you somewhere beautiful.

Don't avoid what you feel, because emotions are what make life worth living—without them, everything would feel empty and dull.

Think about it. <3

9 79 88 99 6 1 2 3 2 9